THE SOUND OF A VOICE

BY
DAVID HENRY HWANG

★

★

DRAMATISTS
PLAY SERVICE
INC.

NOTE ON BILLING

SPECIAL NOTE ON SONGS/RECORDINGS

THE SOUND OF A VOICE (on a double bill with THE HOUSE OF SLEEPING BEAUTIES and under the omnibus title of SOUND AND BEAUTY) was presented by Joseph Papp at the New York Shakespeare Festival Public Theater, in New York City, where it opened on November 6, 1983, with the following cast:

MAN .... John Lone
WOMAN .... Natsuko Ohama

(Movement by Ching Valdes and Elizabeth Fong Sung)

Direction was by John Lone, assisted by Lenore Kletter; Scenery by Andrew Jackness; Lighting by John Giscondi; Costumes by Lydia Tanii; Wigs & make-up by Marlies Vallant; music composed by Lucia Hwong. Jason Steven Cohen was associate producer.

CHARACTERS
MAN — fifties, Japanese
WOMAN — fifties, Japanese

SYNOPSIS OF SCENES
Scene one: Evening
Scene two: Dawn
Scene three: Day
Scene four: Night
Scene five: Day
Scene six: Night
Scene seven: Morning
Scene eight: Day
Scene nine: Night

SETTING
WOMAN's house, in a remote corner of a forest

NOTE ON INCIDENTAL MUSIC

Incidental music composed by Lucia Hwong for the New York productions of "Sound of a Voice" and "House of Sleeping Beauties" is available in reel to reel or cassette tape format. For rental please contact:

Harold Orenstein P.C.
157 West 57th Street
Room 500
New York, N.Y. 10019
(212) 247-6460

THE SOUND OF A VOICE

Woman pours tea for Man. Man rubs himself, trying to get warm.

MAN. You're very kind to take me in.
WOMAN. This is a remote corner of the world. Guests are rare.
MAN. The tea—you pour it well.
WOMAN. No.
MAN. The sound it makes—in the cup—very soothing.
WOMAN. That is the tea's skill, not mine. (*She hands the cup to him.*) May I get you something else? Rice, perhaps?
MAN. No.
WOMAN. And some vegetables?
MAN. No, thank you.
WOMAN. Fish? (*Pause.*) It is at least two days walk to the nearest village. I saw no horse. You must be very hungry. You would do a great honor to dine with me. Guests are rare.
MAN. Thank you.
WOMAN. (*Woman gets up, leaves. Man holds the cup in his hands, using it to warm himself. He gets up, walks around the room. It is sparsely furnished, drab, except for one shelf on which stands a vase of brightly colored flowers. The flowers stand out in sharp contrast to the starkness of the room. Slowly, he reaches out towards them. He touches them. Quickly, he takes one of the flowers from the vase, hides it in his clothes. He returns to where he had sat previously. He waits. Woman re-enters. She carries a tray with food.*) Please. Eat. It will give me great pleasure.
MAN. This—this is magnificent.
WOMAN. Eat.
MAN. Thank you. (*He motions for Woman to join him.*)
WOMAN. No, thank you.

MAN. This is wonderful. The best I've tasted.
WOMAN. You are reckless in your flattery. But anything you say, I will enjoy hearing. It's not even the words. It's the sound of a voice, the way it moves through the air.
MAN. How long has it been since you last had a visitor? (*Pause.*)
WOMAN. I don't know.
MAN. Oh?
WOMAN. I lose track. Perhaps five months ago, perhaps ten years, perhaps yesterday. I don't consider time when there is no voice in the air. It's pointless. Time begins with the entrance of a visitor, and ends with his exit.
MAN. And in between? You don't keep track of the days? You can't help but notice —
WOMAN. Of course I notice.
MAN. Oh.
WOMAN. I notice, but I don't keep track. (*Pause.*) May I bring out more?
MAN. More? No. No. This was wonderful.
WOMAN. I have more.
MAN. Really — the best I've had.
WOMAN. You must be tired. Did you sleep in the forest last night?
MAN. Yes.
WOMAN. Or did you not sleep at all?
MAN. I slept.
WOMAN. Where?
MAN. By a waterfall. The sound of the water put me to sleep. It rumbled like the sounds of a city. You see, I can't sleep in too much silence. It scares me. It makes me feel that I have no control over what is about to happen.
WOMAN. I feel the same way.
MAN. But you live here — alone?
WOMAN. Yes.
MAN. It's so quiet here. How can you sleep?
WOMAN. Tonight, I'll sleep. I'll lie down in the next room, and hear your breathing through the wall, and fall asleep shamelessly. There will be no silence.
MAN. You're very kind to let me stay here.
WOMAN. This is yours. (*She unrolls a mat; there is a beautiful de-*

sign of a flower on the mat. The flower looks exactly like the flowers in the vase.)
MAN. Did you make it yourself?
WOMAN. Yes. There is a place to wash outside.
MAN. Thank you.
WOMAN. Goodnight.
MAN. Goodnight. (*Man starts to leave.*)
WOMAN. May I know your name?
MAN. No. I mean, I would rather not say. If I gave you a name, it would only be made-up. Why should I deceive you? You are too kind for that.
WOMAN. Then what should I call you? Perhaps—"Man Who Fears Silence?"
MAN. How about, "Man Who Fears Women?"
WOMAN. That name is much too common.
MAN. And you?
WOMAN. Yokiko.
MAN. That's your name?
WOMAN. It's what you may call me.
MAN. Goodnight, Yokiko. You are very kind.
WOMAN. You are very smart. Goodnight. (*Man exits. Hanako goes to the mat. She tidies it, brushes it off. She goes to the vase. She picks up the flowers, studies them. She carries them out of the room with her. Man re-enters. He takes off his outer clothing. He glimpses the spot where the vase used to sit. He reaches into his clothing, pulls out the stolen flower. He studies it. He puts it underneath his head as he lies down to sleep, like a pillow. He starts to fall asleep. Suddenly, a start. He picks up his head. He listens.*)

SCENE TWO

Dawn. Man is getting dressed. Woman enters with food.

WOMAN. Good morning.
MAN. Good morning, Yokiko.
WOMAN. You weren't planning to leave?
MAN. I have quite a distance to travel today.
WOMAN. Please. (*She offers him food.*)
MAN. Thank you.

WOMAN. May I ask where you're travelling to?
MAN. It's far.
WOMAN. I know this region well.
MAN. Oh? Do you leave the house often?
WOMAN. I used to. I used to travel a great deal. I know the region from those days.
MAN. You probably wouldn't know the place I'm headed.
WOMAN. Why not?
MAN. It's new. A new village. It didn't exist in "those days." (*Pause.*)
WOMAN. I thought you said you wouldn't deceive me.
MAN. I didn't. You don't believe me, do you?
WOMAN. No.
MAN. Then I didn't deceive you. I'm travelling. That much is true.
WOMAN. Are you in such a hurry?
MAN. Travelling is a matter of timing. Catching the light. (*Woman exits; Man finishes eating, puts down his bowl. Woman re-enters with the vase of flowers.*) Where did you find those? They don't grow native around these parts, do they?
WOMAN. No; they've all been brought in. They were brought in by visitors. Such as yourself. They were left here. In my custody.
MAN. But—they look so fresh, so alive.
WOMAN. I take care of them. They remind me of the people and places outside this house.
MAN. May I touch them?
WOMAN. Certainly.
MAN. These have just blossomed.
WOMAN. No; they were in bloom yesterday. If you'd noticed them before, you would know that.
MAN. You must have received these very recently. I would guess—within five days.
WOMAN. I don't know. But I wouldn't trust your estimate. It's all in the amount of care you show to them. I create a world which is outside the realm of what you know.
MAN. What do you do?
WOMAN. I can't explain. Words are too inefficient. It takes hundreds of words to describe a single act of caring. With hun-

dreds of acts, words become irrelevant. (*Pause.*) But perhaps
you can stay.
MAN. How long?
WOMAN. As long as you'd like.
MAN. Why?
WOMAN. To see how I care for them.
MAN. I *am* tired.
WOMAN. Rest.
MAN. The light?
WOMAN. It will return.

SCENE THREE

*Man is carrying chopped wood. He is stripped to the waist.
Woman enters.*

WOMAN. You're very kind to do that for me.
MAN. I enjoy it, you know. Chopping wood. It's clean. No
questions. You take your axe, you stand up the log, you aim —
pow! — you either hit it or you don't. Success or failure.
WOMAN. You seem to have been very successful today.
MAN. Why shouldn't I be? It's a beautiful day. I can see to
those hills. The trees are cool. The sun is gentle. Ideal. If a man
can't be successful on a day like this, he might as well kick the
dust up into his own face. (*Man notices Woman staring at him. Man
pats his belly, looks at her.*) Protection from falls.
WOMAN. What? (*Man pinches his belly, showing some fat.*) Oh.
Don't be silly. (*Man begins slapping the fat on his belly to a rhythm.*)
MAN. Listen — I can make music — see? — that wasn't always
possible. But now — that I've developed this — whenever I need
entertainment.
WOMAN. You shouldn't make fun of your body.
MAN. Why not? I saw you. You were staring.
WOMAN. I wasn't making fun. (*Man inflates his cheeks.*) I was
just — stop that!
MAN. Then why were you staring?
WOMAN. I was —
MAN. Laughing?

9

WOMAN. No.

MAN. Well?

WOMAN. I was—Your body. It's . . . strong. (*Pause.*)

MAN. People say that. But they don't know. I've heard that age brings wisdom. That's a laugh. The years don't accumulate here. They accumulate here. (*Pause; he pinches his belly.*) But today is a day to be happy, right? The woods. The sun. Blue. It's a happy day. I'm going to chop wood.

WOMAN. There's nothing left to chop. Look.

MAN. Oh. I guess . . . that's it.

WOMAN. Sit. Here.

MAN. But—

WOMAN. There's nothing left. (*Man sits; Woman stares at his belly.*) Learn to love it.

MAN. Don't be ridiculous.

WOMAN. Touch it.

MAN. It's flabby.

WOMAN. It's strong.

MAN. It's weak.

WOMAN. And smooth.

MAN. Do you mind if I put on my shirt?

WOMAN. Of course not. Shall I get it for you?

MAN. No. No. Just sit there. (*Man starts to put on his shirt. He pauses, studies his body.*) You think it's cute, huh?

WOMAN. I think you should learn to love it. (*Man pats his belly, talks to it.*)

MAN. (*To belly:*) You're okay, sir. You hang onto my body like a great horseman.

WOMAN. Not like that.

MAN. (*Ibid.*) You're also faithful. You'll never leave me for another man.

WOMAN. No.

MAN. What do you want me to say? (*Woman walks over to Man. She touches his belly with her hand. They look at each other.*)

SCENE FOUR

Night. Man is alone. Flowers are gone from stand. Mat is unrolled. Man lies on it, sleeping. Suddenly, he starts. He lifts up

10

his head. He listens. Silence. He goes back to sleep. Another start. He lifts up his head, strains to hear. Slowly, we begin to make out the strains of a single shakuhachi playing a haunting line. It is very soft. He strains to hear it. The instrument slowly fades out. He waits for it to return, but it does not. He takes out the stolen flower. He stares into it.

SCENE FIVE

Day. Woman is cleaning, while Man relaxes. She is on her hands and knees, scrubbing. She is dressed in a simple outfit, for working. Her hair is tied back. Man is sweating. He has not, however, removed his shirt.

MAN. I heard your playing last night.
WOMAN. My playing?
MAN. Shakuhachi.
WOMAN. Oh.
MAN. You played very softly. I had to strain to hear it. Next time, don't be afraid. Play out. Fully. Clear. It must've been very beautiful, if only I could've heard it clearly. Why don't you play for me sometime?
WOMAN. I'm very shy about it.
MAN. Why?
WOMAN. I play for my own satisfaction. That's all. It's something I developed on my own. I don't know if it's at all acceptable by outside standards.
MAN. Play for me. I'll tell you.
WOMAN. No; I'm sure you're too knowledgeable in the arts.
MAN. Who? Me?
WOMAN. You being from the city and all.
MAN. I'm ignorant, believe me.
WOMAN. I'd play, and you'd probably bite your cheek.
MAN. Ask me a question about music. Any question. I'll answer incorrectly. I guarantee it.
WOMAN. Look at this.
MAN. What?
WOMAN. A stain.
MAN. Where?

11

WOMAN. Here? See? I can't get it out.
MAN. Oh. I hadn't noticed it before.
WOMAN. I notice it every time I clean.
MAN. Here. Let me try.
WOMAN. Thank you.
MAN. Ugh. It's tough.
WOMAN. I know.
MAN. How did it get here?
WOMAN. It's been there as long as I've lived here.
MAN. I hardly stand a chance. (*Pause.*) But I'll try. Uh—one—two—three—four! One—two—three—four! See, you set up . . . gotta set up . . . a rhythm—two—three—four. Like fighting! Like battle! One—two—three—four! Used to practice with a rhythm . . . beat . . . battle! Yes! (*The stain starts to fade away.*) Look—it's—yes!—whoo!—there it goes—got the sides—the edges—yes!—fading quick—fading away—ooo—here we come —towards the center—to the heart—two—three—four—slow —slow death—tough—dead! (*Man rolls over in triumphant laughter.*)
WOMAN. Dead.
MAN. I got it! I got it! Whoo! A little rhythm! All it took! Four! Four!
WOMAN. Thank you.
MAN. I didn't think I could do it—but there—it's gone—I did it!
WOMAN. Yes. You did.
MAN. And you—you were great.
WOMAN. No—I was carried away.
MAN. We were a team! You and me!
WOMAN. I only provided encouragement.
MAN. You were great! You were! (*Man grabs Woman. Pause.*)
WOMAN. It's gone. Thank you. Would you like to hear me play shakuhachi?
MAN. Yes I would.
WOMAN. I don't usually play for visitors. It's so . . . I'm not sure. I developed it—all by myself—in times when I was alone. I heard nothing—no human voice. So I learned to play shakuhachi. I tried to make these sounds resemble the human voice. The shakuhachi became my weapon. To ward off the air. It kept me from choking on many a silent evening.
MAN. I'm here. You can hear my voice.

WOMAN. Speak again.
MAN. I will.

Scene Six

Night. Man is sleeping. Suddenly, a start. He lifts his head up. He listens. Silence. He strains to hear. The shakuhachi melody rises up once more. This time, however, it becomes louder and more clear than before. He gets up. He cannot tell from what direction the music is coming. He walks around the room, putting his ear to different places in the wall, but he cannot locate the sound. It seems to come from all directions at once, as omnipresent as the air. Slowly, he moves towards the wall with the sliding panel through which the Woman enters and exits. He puts his ear against it, thinking the music may be coming from there. Slowly, he slides the door open just a crack, ever so carefully. He peeks through the crack. As he peeks through, the Upstage wall of the set becomes transparent, and through the scrim, we are able to see what he sees. Woman is Upstage of the scrim. She is tending a room filled with potted and vased flowers of all variety. The lushness and beauty of the room Upstage of the scrim stands out in stark contrast to the barrenness of the main set. She is also transformed. She is a young woman. She is beautiful. She wears a brightly colored kimono. Man observes this scene for a long time. He then slides the door shut. The scrim returns to opaque. The music continues. He returns to his mat. He picks up the stolen flower. It is brown and wilted, dead. He looks at it. The music slowly fades out.

Scene Seven

Morning. Man is half-dressed. He is practicing sword maneuvers. He practices with the feel of a man whose spirit is willing, but the flesh is inept. He tries to execute deft movements, but is dissatisfied with his efforts. He curses himself, and returns to basic exercises. Suddenly, he feels something buzzing around his neck — a mosquito. He slaps his neck, but misses it. He sees it flying near him. He swipes at it with his sword. He keeps missing. Finally, he thinks he's hit it. He runs over, kneels down to recover the fallen insect. He picks up two halves of a mosquito on two different fingers. Woman enters the room. She looks as she normally does. She is carrying a vase of flowers, which she places on its shelf.

MAN. Look.
WOMAN. I'm sorry?
MAN. Look.
WOMAN. What? (*He brings over the two halves of mosquito to show her.*)
MAN. See?
WOMAN. Oh.
MAN. I hit it — chop!
WOMAN. These are new forms of target practice?
MAN. Huh? Well — yes — in a way.
WOMAN. You seem to do well at it.
MAN. Thank you. For last night. I heard your shakuhachi. It was very loud, strong — good tone.
WOMAN. Did you enjoy it? I wanted you to enjoy it. If you wish, I'll play it for you every night.
MAN. Every night!
WOMAN. If you wish.
MAN. No — I don't — I don't want you to treat me like a baby.
WOMAN. What? I'm not.
MAN. Oh, yes. Like a baby. Who you must feed in the middle of the night or he cries. Waaah! Waaah!
WOMAN. Stop that!
MAN. You need your sleep.
WOMAN. I don't mind getting up for you. (*Pause.*) I would enjoy playing for you. Every night. While you sleep. It will make me feel — like I'm shaping your dreams. I go through long stretches when there is no one in my dreams. It's terrible. During those times, I avoid my bed as much as possible. I paint. I weave. I play shakuhachi. I sit on mats and rub powder into my face. Anything to keep from facing a bed with no dreams. It is like sleeping on ice.

MAN. What do you dream of now?
WOMAN. Last night—I dreamt of you. I don't remember what happened. But you were very funny. Not in a mocking way. I wasn't laughing at you. But you made me laugh. And you were very warm. I remember that. (*Pause.*) What do you remember about last night?
MAN. Just your playing. That's all. I got up, listened to it, and went back to sleep. (*Man gets up, resumes practicing with his sword.*)
WOMAN. Another mosquito bothering you?
MAN. Just practicing. Ah! Weak! Too weak! I tell you, it wasn't always like this. I'm telling you, there were days when I could chop the fruit from a tree without ever taking my eyes off the ground. (*He continues practicing.*) You ever use one of these?
WOMAN. I've had to pick one up, yes.
MAN. Oh?
WOMAN. You forget—I live alone—out here—there is . . . not much to sustain me but what I manage to learn myself. It wasn't really a matter of choice.
MAN. I used to be very good, you know. Perhaps I can give you some pointers.
WOMAN. I'd really rather not.
MAN. C'mon—a woman like you—you're absolutely right. You need to know how to defend yourself.
WOMAN. As you wish.
MAN. Do you have something to practice with?
WOMAN. Yes. Excuse me. (*She exits. He practices more. She re-enters with two wooden sticks. He takes one of them.*) Will these do?
MAN. Nice. Now, show me what you can do.
WOMAN. I'm sorry?
MAN. Run up and hit me.
WOMAN. Please.
MAN. Go on—I'll block it.
WOMAN. I feel so . . . undignified.
MAN. Go on. (*She hits him playfully with stick.*) Not like that!
WOMAN. I'll try to be gentle.
MAN. What?
WOMAN. I don't want to hurt you.
MAN. You won't—Hit me! (*Woman charges at Man, quickly, deftly. She scores a hit.*) Oh!
WOMAN. Did I hurt you?

MAN. No—you were—let's try that again. (*They square off again. Woman rushes forward. She appears to attempt a strike. He blocks that apparent strike, which turns out to be a feign. She scores.*) Huh?
WOMAN. Did I hurt you? I'm sorry.
MAN. No.
WOMAN. I hurt you.
MAN. No.
WOMAN. Do you wish to hit me?
MAN. No.
WOMAN. Do you want me to try again?
MAN. No.
WOMAN. Thank you.
MAN. Just practice there—by yourself—let me see you run through some maneuvers.
WOMAN. Must I?
MAN. Yes! Go! (*She goes to an open area.*) My greatest strength was always as a teacher. (*Woman executes a series of deft movements. Her whole manner is transformed. Man watches with increasing amazement. Her movements end. She regains her submissive manner.*)
WOMAN. I'm so embarrassed. My skills—they're so—inappropriate. I look like a man.
MAN. Where did you learn that?
WOMAN. There is much time to practice here.
MAN. But you—the techniques.
WOMAN. I don't know what's fashionable in the outside world. (*Pause.*) Are you unhappy?
MAN. No.
WOMAN. Really?
MAN. I'm just . . . surprised.
WOMAN. You think it's unbecoming for a woman.
MAN. No, no. Not at all.
WOMAN. You want to leave.
MAN. No!
WOMAN. All visitors do. I know. I've met many. They say they'll stay. And they do. For a while. Until they see too much. Or they learn something new. There are boundaries outside of which visitors do not want to see me step. Only who knows what those boundaries are? Not I. They change with every visitor. You have to be careful not to cross them, but you never know where they are. And one day, inevitably, you step outside the

lines. The visitor knows. You don't. You didn't know that you'd
done anything different. You thought it was just another part of
you. The visitor sneaks away. The next day, you learn that you
had stepped outside his heart. I'm afraid you've seen too much.
MAN. There are stories.
WOMAN. What?
MAN. People talk.
WOMAN. Where? We're two days from the nearest village.
MAN. Word travels.
WOMAN. What are you talking about?
MAN. There are stories about you. I heard them. They say
that your visitors never leave this house.
WOMAN. That's what you heard?
MAN. They say you imprison them.
WOMAN. Then you were a fool to come here.
MAN. Listen.
WOMAN. Me? Listen? You. Look! Where are these prison-
ers? Have you seen any?
MAN. They told me you were very beautiful.
WOMAN. Then they are blind as well as ignorant.
MAN. You are.
WOMAN. What?
MAN. Beautiful.
WOMAN. Stop that! My skin feels like seaweed.
MAN. I didn't realize it at first. I must confess — I didn't. But
over these few days — your face has changed for me. The shape
of it. The feel of it. The color. All changed. I look at you now,
and I'm no longer sure you are the same woman who had poured
tea for me just a week ago. And because of that I remembered
— how little I know about a face that changes in the night.
(*Pause.*) Have you heard those stories?
WOMAN. I don't listen to old wives' tales.
MAN. But have you heard them?
WOMAN. Yes. I've heard them. From other visitors — young
— hotblooded — or old — who came here because they were told
great glory was to be had by killing the witch in the woods.
MAN. I was told that no man could spend time in this house
without falling in love.
WOMAN. Oh? So why did you come? Did you wager gold that
you could come out untouched? The outside world is so flatter-

ing to me. And you—are you like the rest? Passion passing through your heart so powerfully that you can't hold onto it?
MAN. No! I'm afraid!
WOMAN. Of what?
MAN. Sometimes—when I look into the flowers, I think I hear a voice—from inside—a voice beneath the petals. A human voice.
WOMAN. What does it say? "Let me out?"
MAN. No. Listen. It hums. It hums with the peacefulness of one who is completely imprisoned.
WOMAN. I understand that if you listen closely enough, you can hear the ocean.
MAN. No. Wait. Look at it. See the layers? Each petal—hiding the next. Try and see where they end. You can't. Follow them down, further down, around—and as you come down—faster and faster—the breeze picks up. The breeze becomes a wail. And in that rush of air—in the silent midst of it—you can hear a voice. (*Woman grabs flower from Man.*)
WOMAN. So, you believe I water and prune my lovers? How can you be so foolish? (*She snaps the flower in half, at the stem. She throws it to the ground.*) Do you come only to leave again? To take a chunk of my heart, then leave with your booty on your belt, like a prize? You say that I imprison hearts in these flowers? Well, bits of my heart are trapped with travellers across this land. I can't even keep track. So kill me. If you came here to destroy a witch, kill me now. I can't stand to have it happen again.
MAN. I won't leave you.
WOMAN. I believe you. (*She looks at the flower that she has broken, bends to pick it up. He touches her. They embrace.*)

SCENE EIGHT

Day. Woman wears a simple undergarment, over which she is donning a brightly colored kimono, the same one we saw her wearing U. of the scrim. Man stands apart.

WOMAN. I can't cry. I don't have the capacity. Right from birth, I didn't cry. My mother and father were shocked. They thought they'd given birth to a ghost, a demon. Sometimes I've

18

thought myself that. When great sadness has welled up inside me, I've prayed for a means to release the pain from my body. But my prayers went unanswered. The grief remained inside me. It would sit like water, still. (*Pause; she models her kimono.*) Do you like it?
MAN. Yes, it's beautiful.
WOMAN. I wanted to wear something special today.
MAN. It's beautiful. Excuse me. I must practice.
WOMAN. Shall I get you something?
MAN. No.
WOMAN. Some tea, maybe?
MAN. No. (*Man resumes swordplay.*)
WOMAN. Perhaps later today—perhaps we can go out—just around here. We can look for flowers.
MAN. All right.
WOMAN. We don't have to.
MAN. No. Let's.
WOMAN. I just thought if—
MAN. Fine. Where do you want to go?
WOMAN. There are very few recreational activities around here, I know.
MAN. All right. We'll go this afternoon. (*Pause.*)
WOMAN. Can I get you something?
MAN. (*Turning around.*) What?
WOMAN. You might be—
MAN. I'm not hungry or thirsty or cold or hot.
WOMAN. Then what are you?
MAN. Practicing. (*Man resumes practicing; Woman exits. As soon as she exits, he rests. He sits down. He examines his sword. He runs his finger along the edge of it. He takes the tip, runs it against the soft skin under his chin. He places the sword on the ground with the tip pointed directly upwards. He keeps it from falling by placing the tip under his chin. He experiments with different degrees of pressure. Woman re-enters. She sees him in this precarious position. She jerks his head upward; the sword falls.*)
WOMAN. Don't do that!
MAN. What?
WOMAN. You can hurt yourself!
MAN. I was practicing!
WOMAN. You were playing!

MAN. I was practicing!
WOMAN. It's dangerous.
MAN. What do you take me for — a child?
WOMAN. Sometimes wise men do childish things.
MAN. I knew what I was doing!
WOMAN. It scares me.
MAN. Don't be ridiculous. (*He reaches for the sword again.*)
WOMAN. Don't! Don't do that!
MAN. Get back! (*He places the sword back in its previous position, suspended between the floor and his chin, upright.*)
WOMAN. But —
MAN. Sssssh!
WOMAN. I wish —
MAN. Listen to me! The slightest shock, you know — the slightest shock — surprise — it might make me jerk or — something — and then . . . So you must be perfectly still and quiet.
WOMAN. But I —
MAN. Sssssh! (*Silence.*) I learned this exercise from a friend — I can't even remember his name — good swordsman — many years ago. He called it his meditation position. He said, like this, he could feel the line between this world and the others because he rested on it. If he saw something in another world that he liked better, all he would have to do is let his head drop, and he'd be there. Simple. No fuss. One day, they found him with the tip of his sword run clean out the back of his neck. He was smiling. I guess he saw something he liked. Or else he'd fallen asleep.
WOMAN. Stop that.
MAN. Stop what?
WOMAN. Tormenting me.
MAN. I'm not.
WOMAN. Take it away!
MAN. You don't have to watch, you know.
WOMAN. Do you want to die that way — an accident?
MAN. I was doing this before you came in.
WOMAN. If you do, all you need to do is tell me.
MAN. What?
WOMAN. I can walk right over. Lean on the back of your head.
MAN. Don't try to threaten —
WOMAN. Or jerk your sword up.

MAN. Or scare me. You can't threaten —
WOMAN. I'm not. But if that's what you want.
MAN. You can't threaten me. You wouldn't do it.
WOMAN. Oh?
MAN. Then I'd be gone. You wouldn't let me leave that easily.
WOMAN. Yes, I would.
MAN. You'd be alone.
WOMAN. No. I'd follow you. Forever. (*Pause.*) Now, let's stop this nonsense.
MAN. No! I can do what I want! Don't come any closer!
WOMAN. Then release your sword.
MAN. Come any closer and I'll drop my head.
WOMAN. (*Woman slowly approaches Man. She grabs the hilt of the sword. She looks into his eyes. She pulls it out from under his chin.*) There will be no more of this. (*She exits with the sword. He starts to follow her, then stops. He touches under his chin. On his finger, he finds a drop of blood.*)

SCENE NINE

Night. Man is leaving the house. He is just about out, when he hears a shakuhachi playing. He looks around, trying to locate the sound. Woman appears in the doorway to the outside. Shakuhachi slowly fades out.

WOMAN. It's time for you to go?
MAN. Yes. I'm sorry.
WOMAN. You're just going to sneak out? A thief in the night? A frightened child?
MAN. I care about you.
WOMAN. You express it strangely.
MAN. I leave in shame because it is proper. (*Pause.*) I came seeking glory.
WOMAN. To kill me? You can say it. You'll be surprised at how little I blanche. As if you'd said, "I came for a bowl of rice," or "I came seeking love" or "I came to kill you."
MAN. Weakness. All weakness. Too weak to kill you. Too weak to kill myself. Too weak to do anything but sneak away in shame. (*Woman brings out Man's sword.*)

21

WOMAN. Were you even planning to leave without this? (*He takes sword.*) Why not stay here?
MAN. I can't live with someone who's defeated me.
WOMAN. I never thought of defeating you. I only wanted to take care of you. To make you happy. Because that made me happy and I was no longer alone.
MAN. You defeated me.
WOMAN. Why do you think that way?
MAN. I came here with a purpose. The world was clear. You changed the shape of your face, the shape of my heart — rearranged everything — created a world where I could do nothing.
WOMAN. I only tried to care for you.
MAN. I guess that was all it took. (*Pause.*)
WOMAN. You still think I'm a witch. Just because old women gossip. You are so cruel. Once you arrived, there were only two possibilities: I would die or you would leave. (*Pause.*) If you believe I'm a witch, then kill me. Rid the province of one more evil.
MAN. I can't —
WOMAN. Why not? If you believe that about me, then it's the right thing to do.
MAN. You know I can't.
WOMAN. Then stay.
MAN. Don't try and force me.
WOMAN. I won't force you to do anything. (*Pause.*) All I wanted was an escape — for both of us. The sound of a human voice — the simplest thing to find, and the hardest to hold onto. This house — my loneliness is etched into the walls. Kill me, but don't leave. Even in death, my spirit would rest here and be comforted by your presence.
MAN. Force me to stay.
WOMAN. I won't. (*Man starts to leave.*) Beware.
MAN. What?
WOMAN. The ground on which you walk is weak. It could give way at any moment. The crevice beneath is dark.
MAN. Are you talking about death? I'm ready to die.
WOMAN. Fear for what is worse than death.
MAN. What?
WOMAN. Falling. Falling through the darkness. Waiting to hit the ground. Picking up speed. Waiting for the ground. Fall-

ing faster. Falling alone. Waiting. Falling. Waiting. Falling. (*Woman wails and runs out through the door to her room. Man stands, confused, not knowing what to do. He starts to follow her, then hesitates, and rushes out the door to the outside. Silence. Slowly, he re-enters from the outside. He looks for her in the main room. He goes slowly towards the panel to her room. He throws down his sword. He opens the panel. He goes inside. He comes out. He unrolls his mat. He sits on it, cross-legged. He looks out into space. He notices near him a shakuhachi. He picks it up. He begins to blow into it. He tries to make sounds. He continues trying through the end of the play. The Upstage scrim lights up. Upstage, we see the Woman. She is young. She is hanging from a rope suspended from the roof. She has hung herself. Around her, are scores of vases with flowers in them whose blossoms have been blown off. Only the stems remain in the vases. Around her swirl the thousands of petals from the flowers. They fill the Upstage scrim area like a blizzard of color. Man continues to attempt to play. Lights fade to black.*)

PROPERTY LIST

Teapot & cups
Vase of flowers
Trays of food (2)
Sleeping mat, with flower design
Chopped wood
Scrub brush & pail
Pots & vases of flowers
Sword
Long wooden sticks (2)